KN★W YOUR RIGHTS!

A Modern Kid's Guide to the American Constitution

LAURA BARCELLA

STERLING CHILDREN'S BOOKS
New York

An Imprint of Sterling Publishing Co., Inc.
1166 Avenue of the Americas
New York, NY 10036

ISBN 978-1-4549-2854-6

Distributed in Canada by Sterling Publishing Co., Inc.
c/o Canadian Manda Group, 664 Annette Street
Toronto, Ontario M6S 2C8, Canada
Distributed in the United Kingdom by GMC Distribution Services
Castle Place, 166 High Street, Lewes, East Sussex BN7 1XU, England
Distributed in Australia by NewSouth Books
45 Beach Street, Coogee NSW 2034, Australia

For information about custom editions, special sales, and premium and corporate purchases, please contact Sterling Special Sales at 800-805-5489 or specialsales@sterlingpublishing.com.

Manufactured in Canada

Lot #:
2 4 6 8 10 9 7 5 3 1

12/17

sterlingpublishing.com

Cover design by Irene Vandervoort
Interior design by Lorie Pagnozzi
All illustrations by Jane Sanders

CONTENTS

KNOW YOUR RIGHTS!

PART ONE

THE CONSTITUTION: AN OVERVIEW

What Does the Constitution *Do,* Anyway?

America is obviously a pretty awesome country. Not only do we have Disney World, but we've also got boardwalk fries, Wi-Fi, an excess of toy stores, and the wonder that is deep-dish pizza. America was founded on a few basic principles that almost everyone can get behind: equality, liberty, and the right to do what makes you happy. But that doesn't mean you have free rein to do absolutely anything your heart desires. As you probably already know, this cool country of ours is run on laws that dictate what people can and can't do.

You might be thinking: That sounds super strict and boring! But we need laws to keep us safe (and to keep people from pushing us around!). With so many citizens sharing one massive country, things could get pretty chaotic if we didn't have some basic rules in place.

Fast Fact

There are at least 5,000 federal criminal laws in America right now. A federal criminal law is a law that applies to all fifty states. There are other laws that only apply in certain states; those are called state laws.

You're going to hear the term *federal* used throughout this book in different ways. *Federal* basically just means "national"—as in, having to do with the entire country. One way to remember this is to think about how a federal criminal law is a law that applies to the whole country.

If you've ever wondered who made the laws that run this country—and how those laws are enforced—keep reading! This book will also explain to you exactly what YOUR rights are. Because no matter where you live; what race, age, or gender you are; or what religious background you come from, you've got rights—a lot of them, actually. And so does your dad, your best friend, your teacher, and that eccentric guy you see sometimes at the grocery store. We all have rights. Now let's learn a little more about them!

THE U.S. CONSTITUTION: THE WHY, WHO, AND WHAT

Many of the laws we have today were put into place by the Constitution, a document signed way back in 1787 (yep, that's more than 200 years ago). But what *is* the Constitution, and why does it exist in the first place?

Why

The government that we have today didn't exist until the U.S. Constitution was written. But to understand *why* the Constitution was created, we'll need to take a quick stroll down memory lane to a time before America was, well, America as we know it.

THE ORIGINAL THIRTEEN COLONIES

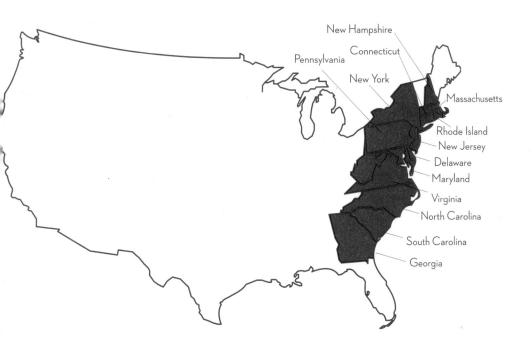

Before the United States became what it is now, it was made up of thirteen colonies ruled by Great Britain. Colonists became more and more upset about how they were being treated under the rule of King George III. Angry with the king's policies and that colonists' concerns weren't being met, small arguments began to turn into big squabbles.

For instance, colonists *hated* the Stamp Act of 1765 that introduced a tax requiring a stamp on printed materials such as newspapers, licenses, and even playing cards. They also hated the Tea Act that put a high tax on tea. Back then, most people were big tea drinkers, so they found this tax extremely outrageous and unfair! In fact, some enraged colonists disliked this tax so much that they dumped more than forty-five tons of tea into the Boston Harbor. By today's standards, the amount of tea they dumped out was worth $1,700,000! (This infamous incident became known as the Boston Tea Party.)

Colonists were desperate for both a new way of life *and* a new government that would represent them. So they began to fight for their freedom from British rule during the American Revolutionary War (or the American Revolution). On July 2, 1776, they formally announced they were cutting ties with Great Britain to form a brand new union—the United States of America. To make it official, they drafted a document called the Declaration of Independence and approved all edits on July 4th. Today, we remember and celebrate this day as the Fourth of July, or Independence Day! The Founding Fathers (leaders of the revolution) signed the document in August. Seven of the most significant Founding Fathers were James Madison, John Adams, Benjamin Franklin, Alexander Hamilton, John Jay, Thomas Jefferson, and George Washington.

After the United States won the war and gained independence, leaders of the Revolution were tasked with the challenge of creating a new government. They knew they wanted a government that was totally different from the unjust rule of King George III. That's why they laid out the Constitution in such a way that the power belonged to the people and that no one person, group, or part of the government could take that power away. This kind of government, in which ordinary people have a voice, is called a *democracy*.

Fun Fact

Hamilton: An American Musical is a hip-hop Broadway musical about Alexander Hamilton, one of the Founding Fathers of the United States and Secretary of the U.S. Treasury.

In 2016, *Hamilton* received sixteen Tony nominations and won eleven, including Best Musical, and was the recipient of the 2016 Grammy Award for Best Musical Theater Album and the 2016 Pulitzer Prize for Drama.

Who

In 1787, delegates from twelve of the thirteen states that existed gathered at a big meeting called the Philadelphia Convention. That event, held in Philadelphia, Pennsylvania, is commonly referred to as the Constitutional Convention, because an important aspect of it was the creation of the U.S. Constitution. Fifty-five delegates at the Convention helped create the Constitution, with thirty-nine actually signing the document.

The Constitution was drafted by a group of men known as the Framers. Some—but not all—of the Framers were also our country's Founding Fathers.

Did You Know?

Before the Constitution was created, a different document called the Articles of Confederation was considered the highest law in the land. It established the role of the government after the United States became independent from Britain, but it proved to be a weak document with little power to get things done. Luckily for everyone, the U.S. Constitution replaced the Articles of Confederation.

What

The Constitution is made up of a bunch of different parts. There's a brief Preamble, which explains the Constitution's meaning and purpose. It reads:

We the People of the United States, in Order to form a more perfect Union, establish Justice, insure domestic Tranquility, provide for the common defence, promote the general Welfare, and secure the Blessings of Liberty to ourselves and our Posterity, do ordain and establish this Constitution for the United States of America.

Who Cares?

The first three words of the Preamble, *We the People*, are a big deal. They're there to show that the new government's purpose is to serve *us*, the American people. Without citizens, a government wouldn't even be necessary! At the time those words were written, this was a pretty groundbreaking concept.

After the Preamble, there are seven Articles and twenty-seven amendments. The Articles are parts of the Constitution that were originally written and signed by the Framers. The amendments are the changes that were added later on.

As a document, the U.S. Constitution serves as the highest law in the land. It separates power between the federal government (the national government) and state governments and lays out the basic civil (human) rights that every American has. Civil rights are the bedrock of our society that guarantee equal opportunity for *all* citizens.

Each state also has its own unique constitution with laws that only pertain to that pocket of the country, but the U.S. Constitution is considered higher than those.

> **We hold these truths to be self-evident, that all men are created equal, that they are endowed by their Creator with certain unalienable Rights, that among these are Life, Liberty and the pursuit of Happiness.**
>
> **—THE DECLARATION OF INDEPENDENCE**

Because America has changed so much over the years—in fact, it's still changing now—the Constitution sometimes has to change to keep up. It evolves as the nation and its people evolve. When the Constitution is altered and a new law is added, that new addition is called an *amendment*. You can probably guess that it's called this because an addition to the Constitution is meant to amend—to fix or improve—what's already there. There are currently twenty-seven amendments; the first ten are the super-important *Bill of Rights*, which will be explored in detail later in this book.

Fun Fact

The U.S. Constitution is the world's longest-lasting written constitution. It's been amended, but never replaced!

Division of Power

The Framers set up the government to have three parts: a *legislative branch*, an *executive branch*, and a *judicial branch*. Outlined in the first three Articles of the Constitution, these branches were designed to ensure that no one person or group could ever gain too much control (remember, the Framers wanted to avoid repeating a King George III situation!). With the power divided three ways, each branch is responsible for certain parts of the government, and together, the branches keep each other's actions in check. This is why this concept is called *checks and balances*.

THE LEGISLATIVE BRANCH (CONSTITUTION ARTICLE I)

The legislative branch is also known as Congress. You've probably heard this word used before! Congress is responsible for creating and passing U.S. laws, and it's made up of two important bodies, or parts: the *Senate* and the *House of Representatives*. The jobs of the Senate and the House of Representatives are to write and vote on new laws called *bills*. To become an official law, a bill must be voted on and approved by the Senate and House of Representatives—*and* signed by the president. This is an example of how the branches check one another; the legislative branch proposes new laws, but the executive branch—led by the president—gives the final approval.

All fifty states are represented in the Senate, with two senators per state, for a total of 100 senators. Each senator serves a six-year term, after which that spot is open again for election. The vice president of the United States is the head of the Senate, but he or she can't vote on bills (unless the final vote on a bill is a tie) because the vice president is also part of the executive branch. In the House of Representatives, there are 435 members, with each state having a different number of representatives based on how many people live in that state. For example, there are more representatives from New York than there are from South Dakota because New York has a higher population. Each representative's term only lasts two years.

How Congress Creates Laws

The cool thing about laws is that they're really only . . . ideas. In other words, every law we currently have in place stems from an idea someone had that was then turned into a bill. That bill eventually was voted into an official law, and . . . voilà, a new law was made!

But to make all that happen, there's a pretty strict process in place. It begins when a person writes a bill explaining the ins and outs of the law being proposed. Literally anyone—even kids—can write a bill, but a member of Congress must champion it in order for it to be voted on. That member of Congress then presents the bill to some other members of Congress, and together they decide whether to reject, accept, or change the bill. If the bill is approved by this group, it is then presented to the House of Representatives. The House of Representatives then debates about the bill section by section, stating why they are for or against it; after that, the House votes on whether to turn that bill into a law. If the majority of the House says yes, then the bill is sent to the Senate. If the majority of the Senate votes yes, then the bill is sent to the president, who either signs the bill into law or uses presidential veto power (the power to reject) to block the bill from becoming a law. (More about vetoes and awesome presidential stuff coming up!) But there's a catch. Even if the president vetoes a bill, Congress can override the veto if at least two-thirds of both the House of Representatives and Senate vote to do so.

The Power to Impeach

Impeachment is serious business. It's what happens when a president is accused of illegal activity such as treason, bribery, or other high crimes and misdemeanors that may ultimately cause him or her to be removed from office. The word *impeach* means to formally accuse a public official of doing something wrong, and one of the House of Representatives' most important jobs is to carry out presidential impeachments.

Think About It

A president gets impeached when it is believed he or she is guilty of a high crime or misdemeanor. What do you think some of those crimes or misdemeanors might be? What do you think they *should* be?

Here's how it works: If a president has done something illegal, a member of the House of Representatives has to file impeachment charges against the president. Then the Senate will have a trial, similar to what happens in a criminal court trial. (A trial is an examination of evidence before a judge in court to determine whether someone is guilty of a crime. Generally, a lawyer represents each side and calls witnesses to offer their sides of the story as evidence or to act as experts on subjects related to the case.)

After the trial, two-thirds of the Senate has to vote to impeach the president for the president to be convicted (declared guilty) and possibly booted from the White House. In any case, even if the president *is* allowed to remain in office, he or she can't ever run for president again. Once a president is impeached and convicted, running again is against the law!

What Other Cool Stuff Can Congress Do?

Members of Congress have other responsibilities besides just hanging out in fancy old buildings and making up laws (just kidding—their jobs are super-important!). Here are some other things Congress can do:

★ **Set the government's budget (how much money the government is allowed to spend)**

★ **Collect taxes**

★ **Oversee trade with other countries**

★ **Create immigration policies (this means deciding who can and cannot enter the country)**

★ **Establish post offices**

★ **Declare war**

★ **Organize and support the military**

Did You Know?

Only two U.S. presidents have ever been formally impeached: Andrew Johnson in 1868 and Bill Clinton in 1998. Richard Nixon resigned before he was formally impeached.

ANDREW JOHNSON was accused of violating the Tenure of Office Act. A new law at the time, the Tenure of Office Act prohibited the president from removing officials appointed by the Senate without approval from the Senate. Johnson was later acquitted (not found guilty), and he stayed in office.

BILL CLINTON was impeached on charges of perjury (telling a lie in court) and obstruction of justice, but the Senate acquitted him also. He stayed in office, too.

RICHARD NIXON is another past president who was in a lot of hot water—though his case is unique. In 1974, a congressional committee brought articles of impeachment against President Nixon following the Watergate scandal. (The Watergate scandal involved spying and sabotage from people on Nixon's team against Nixon's opponents in the 1972 presidential campaign.) The president resigned from office before the House could vote on it, though, so Nixon was not technically impeached.

THE EXECUTIVE BRANCH (CONSTITUTION ARTICLE II)

The executive branch of the government is led by the president, who is considered America's chief executive, or leader. Beneath the president—but also part of the executive branch—are the Executive Office of the President and the presidential cabinet. The Executive Office of the President (EOP) is composed of some of the president's closest advisors. Among a range of different important tasks, the EOP communicates messages from the president to the American people and works with other countries to strengthen ties with those countries. The cabinet is similar to the EOP in that its role is also to aid the president. The cabinet includes the vice president along with the heads of fifteen departments that are each focused on a different subject. These heads advise the president, should he or she need help. For example, if the president, needs help making a decision regarding schools, the head of the Department of Education might be consulted. If the decision in question is related to cows (for whatever reason), the head of the Department of Agriculture might be asked to advise.

In cases in which the president can't serve out the rest of a term in office (say, because of impeachment or death), the vice president has to step into the position.

As mentioned earlier, the president can veto laws that are written by Congress, but the president does a whole bunch besides that! The president acts sort of like the head of a very large company. That's a pretty tough job to have, as you can imagine.

Did You Know?

The president doesn't just do super-important government stuff all the time. Every year, the president hosts a number of fun events at the White House, including an Easter Egg Hunt and the lighting of the National Christmas Tree. Like us, the president is allowed to take breaks from work to enjoy sports, movies, travel, and quality time with friends and family.

When taking office, a president takes an oath to preserve, protect, and defend the Constitution. To run for president, you need to be at least thirty-five years old, be born in the United States or to American parents, and have lived in the United States for at least fourteen years. Presidents are elected every four years in a countrywide election, and each president can stay in office—this means to remain president—for eight years, max.

When someone becomes president, he or she takes this special oath, as written in Article Three of the Constitution:

"I do solemnly swear (or affirm) that I will faithfully execute the Office of President of the United States, and will to the best of my Ability, preserve, protect and defend the Constitution of the United States."

As head of the government, the president meets leaders of other countries and talks about ways they can work together. The president also chooses folks to be ambassadors (or representatives) of the United States in other countries around the world. In a situation in which Congress declares war, the president acts as commander in chief of the armed forces. The president also has the *pardon power*, which is important because it means he or she can excuse people who've been accused of committing federal crimes.

Think About It

The original Cabinet under George Washington was only made up of four secretaries, but now there are *tons* more. Why do you think that might be?

THE JUDICIAL BRANCH (CONSTITUTION ARTICLE III)

The judicial branch of our government refers to our court system. It includes the U.S. Supreme Court and lower federal courts. The Supreme Court is considered the highest court in America. This branch of our government is important because it can sometimes be hard to determine right away whether certain laws go against the Constitution (and are, therefore, considered *unconstitutional*). Some laws fall into a gray area, and let's be honest—the wording of the Constitution *is* pretty complex! As part of the government's judicial branch, the job of the Supreme Court is to *interpret the Constitution* to decide whether certain laws agree with it. Here's an overview of the process:

If someone—as in any ordinary person—questions a law passed by Congress and files a lawsuit that reaches the Supreme Court, it's then the Supreme Court's job to decide whether that law agrees with or violates the Constitution. If the Supreme Court finds that the law does in fact go against the Constitution, then that law is declared unconstitutional and is, from then on, no longer a law.

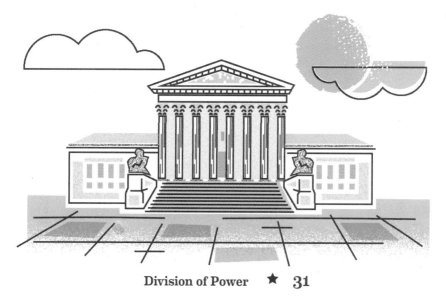

The Supreme Court is made up of nine Supreme Court justices: one chief justice and eight associate justices. Each justice is chosen by the president and approved by the Senate. Throughout the years, hundreds of people have been Supreme Court justices, but only four have been women (Sandra Day O'Connor, Ruth Bader Ginsburg, Sonia Sotomayor, and Elena Kagan).

Each year, thousands of lawyers try to plead cases at the Supreme Court level, but the Supreme Court only decides to hear the most important ones. These cases often have to do with civil rights—rights that justly belong to everyone, so they're relevant to tons of people across the nation. These cases usually receive widespread media attention.

Who Cares? *Brown v. Board of Education of Topeka*

One of the most important Supreme Court rulings ever made was in the 1954 *Brown v. Board of Education of Topeka* case. It had long-standing implications for civil rights and the way race was handled in America. In *Brown v. Board of Education*, the Supreme Court ruled that segregation in public schools—meaning that black kids couldn't attend the same schools as white kids—was unconstitutional, and the practice was banned going forward. This was a huge landmark for civil rights and continues to be relevant today.

FEDERAL VS. STATE
(ARTICLE IV)

When the Constitution was written, power was divvied up between the federal government and the state governments in a system called *federalism*. State governments and the federal government share certain powers, but they also have ones that are all their own. This will be discussed in more detail in the Tenth Amendment section!

CHANGING THE CONSTITUTION
(ARTICLE V)

The only way that the Constitution can change is by adding an amendment. Otherwise, the Constitution is what it is, and the people must abide by it. Other amendments will be explored more deeply later on in this book.

CONSTITUTION AS THE HIGHEST LAW
(ARTICLE VI)

Article VI makes it clear that the Constitution is no joke. It serves as the highest law of the land, and therefore, all government officials—like judges and state representatives, for example—are bound by oath to uphold the Constitution.

MAKING IT OFFICIAL
(ARTICLE VII)

In order to make the Constitution the official governing document of the United States, nine of the original thirteen states had to ratify, or approve, it. Seems simple enough, right? It took almost a year for this to happen! Delaware was the first to approve. Rhode Island was the last.

Here's a cheat sheet for the three branches of government:

EXECUTIVE BRANCH

President

Vice President
and Cabinet

JUDICIAL BRANCH

Supreme Court

Lower Federal Courts

LEGISLATIVE BRANCH

Congress

House of Representatives

Senate

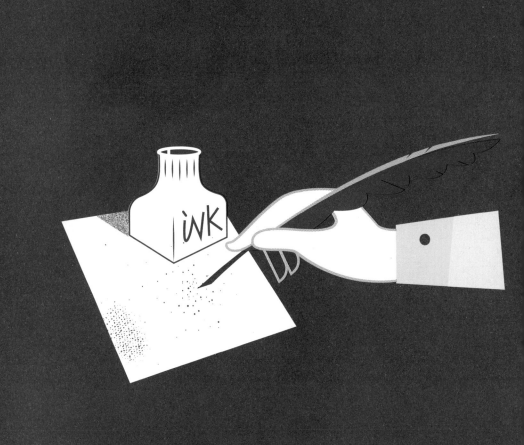

PART TWO

THE BILL OF RIGHTS

Changing the Constitution

The Framers wrote the Constitution a *looooong* time ago. But they were smart folks and they knew the country would evolve over time. So, to accommodate the ever-changing needs of the people, they made it clear in the Constitution that the Constitution *can* change. This way, the document can evolve with the times and stay relevant so it doesn't just become this ancient, dusty text that nobody cares about. In Article V, the Framers arranged a system for amending the Constitution.

Did You Know?

To amend something means to tweak or change it slightly in hopes of making it better.

PASSING AN AMENDMENT: HOW IT'S DONE

In 1787, the Framers decided that in the future, when a change was made to the Constitution, it would be called an *amendment*.

But they didn't want it to be *too* easy to add an amendment. So they agreed upon a formal process:

1. An amendment must first be proposed by two-thirds of Congress.

2. After that, the amendment must be ratified (or approved) by three-quarters of the states.

This process might sound pretty simple, but with all those people involved, it definitely takes time and effort to get an amendment approved. Only twenty-seven amendments have been ratified since the Constitution was first created.

THE BILL OF RIGHTS

A list called the *Bill of Rights* comes immediately after the Articles in the Constitution. The Bill of Rights is the Constitution's first ten amendments—and it's the part of the document you've probably heard the most buzz about. Why? Because the Bill of Rights puts words to the most basic human rights and freedoms that we ALL have as Americans.

These rights include everything from the right to say what you want, pray to whomever you want, and hang out with whomever you wish to share your time with. These rights may seem obvious, but believe it or not, in some countries even today you could get in big trouble for saying something that the government doesn't like. The Bill of Rights was designed to protect us from the whims of the government and remind us that we are a nation of individuals.

Think About It

James Madison (also known as the Father of the Constitution) first proposed the idea of a Bill of Rights to the House of Representatives in 1789, but it wasn't fully ratified until December 1791. Even though tons of citizens agreed that the American people needed a clear list spelling out their rights under the new government, a lot of officials first balked about moving forward with a Bill of Rights. Eleven states had to approve it in order to add it to the Constitution. (Again, we can see how the power is being shared here. James Madison couldn't put the Bill of Rights into effect simply because he said so; he needed approval from other people before moving forward.)

It's important to remember that the Bill of Rights is idealistic, meaning it paints a perfect picture of what America *should* look like. Unfortunately, it wasn't everyone's reality. Back when the Bill of Rights was written, not all Americans had equal rights. For instance, many African-Americans were still being held as slaves, and women still couldn't vote! Social justice strides that tried to fix these issues came later.

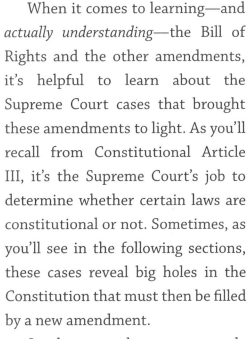

When it comes to learning—and *actually understanding*—the Bill of Rights and the other amendments, it's helpful to learn about the Supreme Court cases that brought these amendments to light. As you'll recall from Constitutional Article III, it's the Supreme Court's job to determine whether certain laws are constitutional or not. Sometimes, as you'll see in the following sections, these cases reveal big holes in the Constitution that must then be filled by a new amendment.

In the next chapter, get ready to learn more about the first ten amendments that make up the Bill of Rights.

Did You Know?

Because public schools receive financial support from the federal government, public school rules and policies must abide by the Constitution and the amendments in the Bill of Rights. You might be surprised, but these requirements do not apply at private schools, because they don't receive funds from the federal government.

The First Ten Amendments

THE FIRST AMENDMENT

Congress shall make no law respecting an establishment of religion, or prohibiting the free exercise thereof; or abridging the freedom of speech, or of the press; or the right of the people peaceably to assemble, and to petition the Government for a redress of grievances.

The First Amendment is a jam-packed doozy of a sentence. It grants people five major rights: freedom of religion, freedom of speech, freedom of the press, the right to assemble in groups, and the right protest against the government.

These may seem specific, but in effect, they do nothing short of guaranteeing your right to life, liberty, and the pursuit of happiness. Which is a pretty big deal! Let's explore this amendment more closely.

Freedom of Religion

There are two parts to our right to the freedom of religion. The first has to do with the "establishment of religion," and it means that the government doesn't have the power to decide there is one official religion for the entire country. For instance, America can never suddenly decide it's ALL Christian or ALL Muslim or ALL Jewish or ALL Scientologist. This part of the amendment protects Americans from being forced to practice the same religion.

The second part of this right gives people the freedom to practice whatever religion they choose, and stops the government, as well as other people, from interfering in their personal religious beliefs.

Freedom of Religion in Action

A landmark case that illustrates the "freedom of religion" part of the First Amendment is *Wisconsin v. Yoder*. In this 1972 case, the Supreme Court decided that Amish students—who are required by their religion to live away from worldly influence—were exempt from, or an exception to, a state law requiring school attendance for all fourteen-to-sixteen year olds. In the case, three Amish parents were prosecuted for not sending their children to high school because they claimed higher education violated their religion. The court said that the benefits of a couple of years of high school education were not great enough to impose such a conflict with the Amish people's freedom to practice their religion *(Wisconsin v. Yoder* 406 U.S. 205 [1972]*)*. Do you agree?

More Examples: In the 1985 case *Lawrence v. Jaffree*, the U.S. Supreme Court struck down an Alabama state law that required prayer in public schools. Since the law had no real purpose other than to put a stamp of approval on one religion, the Court decided it was unconstitutional *(Lawrence v. Jaffree,* 472 U.S. 38 [1985]).

In contrast, in *Board of Education of Westside Community Schools v. Mergens* (1990), the Supreme Court ruled in favor of a law that allowed religious after-school clubs the same access to school facilities as nonreligious clubs. Their reasoning here was that the religious clubs that met on campus were merely *expressing* their beliefs, not promoting them; furthermore, these clubs did not offer school credit, nor were they part of the schoolwide curriculum. *(Board of Education of Westside Community Schools v. Mergens,* 496 U.S. 226 ([1990]).

How Does This Affect Me?

As mentioned, public schools aren't allowed to make students pray during school or promote one specific religion. . . . But they *can* allow students to practice their religion on school grounds when school is not in session. To reiterate, the Supreme Court's reasoning was that, because the schools did not *require* students' participation in the religious clubs, awarded no academic credit to members, and offered no related classes, the religious clubs were considered "non-curriculum related" and could continue to operate on school grounds. (*Non-curriculum related* is not the same as *extracurricular*. The big difference is that for most extracurricular activities, you earn school credit, which means there is academic incentive to join. For non-curriculum activities, there is no credit, so getting involved won't affect your academic standing. All of this to say, if you're interested in starting a religious after-school club at your public school—go for it! You are free to do so.

On a related topic, on public property—like a park—a town can put up symbols involving religious holidays as long as they're mixed in with the nonreligious symbols of the holiday and exist to show the history of the holiday, rather than to just promote a particular religion.

Are there any religious clubs at your school? Besides Santa Clause (a nonreligious symbol), what other symbols—religious or nonreligious—do you see in your neighborhood during the holidays? Do you think there's a balanced mix?

Freedom of Speech

Freedom of speech allows people to state their opinions without fear of punishment. *Speech* can refer to the words coming out of someone's mouth, written words, and other nonverbal forms

of self-expression, some of which do not involve words at all (for example, getting an idea across by wearing certain clothes). There are some limitations, though. For instance, you can't use free speech to make threats, spread obscenity, or incite violence.

Freedom of Speech in Action

Many of the biggest First Amendment cases in the Supreme Court involve students in public schools. For example, in the 1969 case *Tinker v. Des Moines*, the Court ruled in favor of a thirteen-year-old girl named Mary Beth Tinker, who fought the school board on her right to wear black armbands to school in protest of the Vietnam War. (Other students were wearing the bands, too, but Mary Beth and her family were the ones who brought the controversy to the Supreme Court's attention.) The Supreme Court ruled that wearing the armbands was fine and constitutional because it was simply an act of free speech.

This case was incredibly important, because it meant that students didn't lose their First Amendment rights when they stepped onto school grounds and that, unless students' actions seriously interfered with the schools' day-to-day operations, public schools could not censor, or control, students' speech (*Tinker v. Des Moines,* 393 U.S. 503 [1969]).

When, in *Morse v. Frederick*, a student was suspended for holding a banner with a drug-related slogan on it during a school-supervised event, the Supreme Court determined that since the student's banner interfered with the school's antidrug policy, then freedom of speech did *not* apply (*Morse v. Frederick,* 551 U.S. 393 [2007]).

Another situation in which the First Amendment doesn't apply is when a person's speech is designed to cause trouble. The freedom of speech does not apply when words are said to "inflict injury or tend to incite an immediate breach of the peace."

On April 6, 1940, a man named Walter Champlinsky, a Jehovah's Witness, stood in a public place, handing out pamphlets and calling organized religion a "racket." A large crowd gathered. People were causing a scene and blocking roads. After he verbally attacked a city marshal by calling him bad names, Champlinsky was arrested. Champlinsky argued that the arrest violated his freedom of speech. The Court upheld the arrest, explaining that speech is not protected when the content is extremely offensive or designed to cause a major ruckus (*Champlinsky v. New Hampshire,* 315 U.S. 568 [1942]).

Think About It

Many have argued that Champlinsky's speech should have been protected—why do you think this is? What arguments can you think of that would support this point of view?

How Does This Affect Me?

Have you ever exercised your right to the freedom of speech at school? Maybe you have and didn't know it. (If you've ever signed a petition for better cafeteria pizza, then you definitely have.) Are there ways in which you think your school could improve? Maybe not—your school could be perfect! But if there's room for improvement, how can you peacefully voice your opinions?

Freedom of the Press

The First Amendment also ensures that we have freedom of the press. This means that the government can't censor journalists—it can't tell people in the media what to write or say or stop them from reporting the truth. This applies to magazines, newspapers, TV, and other media outlets. The Framers included this because they knew the government could have too much power if it were allowed to block opinions it didn't agree with (or ones that made it look bad), or if it were allowed to keep crucial facts away from the public.

Freedom of the Press in Action

In the 1971 case *New York Times Company v. United States*, President Nixon tried to stop the *New York Times* and the *Washington Post* from publishing the Pentagon Papers, which were important government documents about the U.S. involvement in the Vietnam War. Nixon argued that publishing this material would put America's security at risk, but he didn't really explain why. The Supreme Court disagreed with President Nixon and gave the newspapers the go-ahead to publish the goods (*New York Times Company v. United States*, 403 U.S. 713 [1971]).

"Our liberty depends on freedom of the press, and that cannot be limited without being lost."
—THOMAS JEFFERSON

What About School Newspapers?

School officials *can* regulate student newspapers—in certain situations. In the Supreme Court case *Hazelwood School District v. Kuhlmeier*, students had written articles about teen pregnancy and divorce, and the principal was not cool with that. The students believed their First Amendment rights had been violated, but the Supreme Court ruled that school officials *can* censor students' writing if it was deemed inappropriate in a school context. Why? Because this particular newspaper was part of the educational curriculum *at the school*. It was produced with money from the school district and was part of the school's journalism class. Student newspapers that are funded by a school don't get as much First Amendment protection because their purpose isn't just to share news—it's also to teach students (*Hazelwood District v. Kuhlmeier*, 484 U.S. 260 [1988]).

How Does This Affect Me?

Are you involved in your school newspaper? Have you ever run into trouble with censorship? It might be interesting to ask your journalism teacher if there have ever been any problems with school censorship in the past. Who knows—maybe this could be your next big news story!

Think About It

Do you think the Supreme Court's ruling in the *Hazelwood District v. Kuhlmeier* case was fair or unfair? Explain your answer.

Freedom of Assembly and Protest

The Constitution protects a person's rights to organize or take part in a peaceful assembly (a peaceful protest or gathering), but the government is allowed to put certain limits in place. Those limits can only involve the time, place, or manner of the assembly—but never the *opinions* of the people getting together. For example, people may have to arrange a protest at a certain time of the day, but they're allowed to protest whatever they want.

Freedom of Assembly and Protest in Action

Freedom of assembly means that people can come together to peacefully express their opinions about an issue. For instance, on January 21, 2017, millions of women and men protested as part of the 2017 Women's March. Though people all over the world

organized events and protested on that day, the biggest gathering was in Washington, D.C. People were marching to demand rights for not only women, but also children, minorities, immigrants, and many others whose rights have been historically ignored.

How Does This Affect Me?

Has anyone in your family ever participated in a protest? In what circumstances might a big group assembly or protest be disruptive? What kind of protest do you think you might be interested in attending one day?

THE SECOND AMENDMENT

A well regulated Militia, being necessary to the security of a free State, the right of the people to keep and bear Arms, shall not be infringed.

The Second Amendment gives American citizens the right to bear arms (own guns). This doesn't necessarily apply to you right this second—kids can't legally buy guns, as you probably know. Of course, that doesn't mean guns don't sometimes find their ways into the hands of kids anyway, often causing tragedies to occur. Anyway, because guns are such a massive problem in America (they are used to kill an average of ninety-three people every day), this amendment is really important.

Today, most conversations about the Second Amendment focus on whether it protects the individual's right to bear arms. The tricky thing is, when the Framers drafted the Second Amendment, their concerns were quite different from the concerns we have today. Their worry was that, in certain situations, the government might use soldiers (as in, soldiers with weapons) to control regular citizens by intimidating or frightening them. Under British rule, this was not uncommon. So, to keep this from happening, they made it the right of citizens to bear arms in order to protect themselves from government invasion.

Things are very different these days. Not only is our army highly controlled, but also there is less fear in general of the government using the military as a tool against people.

> "I believe in the Second Amendment. It's there, written on the paper.... But I also believe that we can find ways to reduce gun violence consistent with the Second Amendment."
>
> —PRESIDENT BARACK OBAMA
> (FROM AN EMOTIONAL SPEECH HE GAVE IN 2016
> ABOUT NEW GUN CONTROL MEASURES)

Most of the controversy around the Second Amendment now revolves around gun violence. Some people think that everyone should be able to own a gun just in case we need to protect ourselves from *other* people with guns (bad people with guns); others believe that ownership of firearms needs to be better controlled so that guns aren't available to criminals.

THE THIRD AMENDMENT

No Soldier shall, in time of peace be quartered in any house, without the consent of the Owner, nor in time of war, but in a manner to be prescribed by law.

I'll be honest here: the Third Amendment is probably the least relevant part of the Bill of Rights when it comes to a modern kid's day-to-day life. The Supreme Court has never even had to decide a case based on the Third Amendment! That said, it was pretty important when it was first written.

Basically, the Third Amendment means that you and your

family don't have to turn over your house to members of the military during times of war (or times of peace). Can you believe that in the past, this was a thing that families had to worry about?

See, back when the United States was still under British rule, soldiers were legally allowed to barge in and take over peoples' homes without their consent. This was known as "quartering"—and the Framers wanted to make sure it would never happen again.

THE FOURTH AMENDMENT

The right of the people to be secure in their persons, houses, papers, and effects, against unreasonable searches and seizures, shall not be violated, and no Warrants shall issue, but upon probable cause, supported by Oath or affirmation, and particularly describing the place to be searched, and the persons or things to be seized.

The Fourth Amendment protects people from unreasonable "search and seizure" without a warrant. You might have heard the word *warrant* on cop TV shows—it's a document issued by a court and signed by a judge that gives police permission to search someone's property. The Fourth Amendment explains that police officers can't do these kinds of searches on people's houses, cars, or even their clothes unless they have good reason ("probable cause") to do it.

Probable cause means that there's a pretty good chance that evidence of a crime will be found in a searched area, based on all of the details of the investigation. (Police officers also need probable cause to arrest someone.) A judge won't issue a warrant for officers to search unless they have probable cause.

Probable cause is the logical belief—based on circumstances, but backed up by evidence—that a crime *has been, will be, or is being committed.* Sometimes, it's the Supreme Court's job to determine whether there is probable cause in different scenarios.

Search of a Home

In general, cops can't just barge in and search someone's house without a warrant—it's considered unreasonable. But there *are* some exceptions to this rule. For instance:

★ **When someone in the home gives permission, or consent, to search the home (*Davis v. United States*, 328 U.S. 582 [1946]).**

★ **When the search occurs after a lawful arrest (*United States v. Robinson*, 414 U.S. 218 [1973]).**

★ **When there's probable cause to search, and action must be taken quickly to make sure evidence doesn't get destroyed (*Payton v. New York*, 445 U.S. 573 [1980]).**

★ **When the item being searched for is in plain view of the police officers (*Maryland v. Macon*, 472 U.S. 463 [1985]).**

To determine whether a search violates a person's Fourth Amendment rights, the Supreme Court balances the intrusiveness of the search (for example, a strip search—in which someone is required to remove some or all clothing—is way more intrusive than a locker search!) with the seriousness of the offense (for example, jaywalking is a far less serious offense than stealing). If a person were strip-searched for jaywalking, that would be a pretty big violation of his or her rights!

Searches at School

Students like you and your friends have the Fourth Amendment right not to be needlessly searched at school. But schools also need to keep kids safe and provide a good educational environment. This means school officials can search your things if they have "reasonable suspicion" of criminal activity. They *don't* need probable cause—meaning that they don't need a warrant from a judge; their suspicions alone are enough reason for them to start searching.

Think About It

Do you think it's fair that school officials can search students' belongings without probable cause? How would you feel if that happened to you?

The Fourth Amendment in Action: *New Jersey v. T.L.O.*

In 1984, a fourteen-year-old New Jersey girl was caught smoking at school. When she denied it to her vice principal, the vice principal demanded to look in her purse and found cigarettes, drugs, a bunch of money, and a list of students who owed her money. With this new evidence, a New Jersey court found her guilty of delinquency for drug possession (delinquents are minors, or people under the age of eighteen, who have broken the law). Her lawyers protested this to the Supreme Court, arguing that the search violated the girl's Fourth Amendment rights. When the Supreme Court heard the girl's case, it decided that, while students have a Fourth Amendment right, school officials *can* search their belongings if there's reasonable suspicion of wrongdoing, as the vice principal had in this case, and that they can act on any new evidence discovered in that search (*New Jersey v. T.L.O.*, 469 U.S. 325 [1986]).

Vernonia School District v. Acton

In 1991, a seventh grader named James Acton decided he wanted to play football for his school's team in Vernonia, Oregon. No big deal, right?

When James told his parents this meant he would have to submit to a drug test—as well as random drug tests whenever the school felt like it—his parents were outraged. The school had originally launched their drug-testing policy in response to drug problems (and behavior problems) among other students in the school district. But James was a great student, and his family thought that his rights were being violated.

When James's school wouldn't let him join the sports team after he refused the testing, James and his family sued the school for violating his Fourth Amendment right—they believed the drug-testing policy went against the reasonable-search-and-seizure clause of the Fourth Amendment. But the Supreme Court found that, because the drug testing policy was there to keep students safe and build a better learning environment, the drug policy *was* constitutional (*Vernonia School District v. Acton*, 515 U.S. 646 [1995]).

"I think what we did is being made into a big deal. But I don't think it should be, because I think other people should do things like this also. For our nation to become better, more people have to stand up for the way they think it should be."

—JAMES ACTON

And Another Courtroom Tackles the Fourth Amendment: *Safford Unified School District v. Redding*

In 2009, a thirteen-year-old girl named Savana Redding was strip-searched after one of her fellow students reported that she had ibuprofen with her at Safford Middle School (this was a violation of the school drug policy). Savana then went on to sue the school for violating her Fourth Amendment rights. In *Safford United School District v. Redding*, the Supreme Court agreed that the search did, indeed, violate her rights. While there was enough evidence to justify the search of Savana's bag and outer clothing, the search itself was unreasonable because it was so extreme. While strip searches are allowed in some circumstances, in this instance, there was no evidence that Savana had anything on her besides common over-the-counter painkillers. The Court also took into account that strip searches can be especially difficult for adolescents who are dealing with puberty (*Safford Unified School District v. Redding*, 557 U.S. 364 [2009]).

How Does This Affect Me?

If a school official has "reasonable suspicion" that you've committed a criminal act that could create an unsafe environment or mess with the school's ability to provide students with a good education, he or she can conduct a *reasonable* search of your belongings. The official must have some evidence, though, and can only search places where it is believed you're keeping evidence.

THE FIFTH AMENDMENT

No person shall be held to answer for a capital, or otherwise infamous crime, unless on a presentment or indictment of a Grand Jury, except in cases arising in the land or naval forces, or in the Militia, when in actual service in time of War or public danger; nor shall any person be subject for the same offense to be twice put in jeopardy of life or limb; nor shall be compelled in any criminal case to be a witness against himself, nor

be deprived of life, liberty, or property, without due
process of law; nor shall private property be taken for
public use, without just compensation.

The Framers wanted to protect everyone's rights, including the rights of those accused of a crime.

There are five rights involved in the Fifth Amendment: *the right to a grand jury, the right against double jeopardy, the right to protect oneself against self-incrimination, the right of due process, and the right to eminent domain.*

Because there are a lot of complicated words in this particular amendment, let's discuss what everything means.

Right to a Grand Jury

A grand jury (usually twenty-three members) is a group of regular citizens called to court to determine whether there's enough evidence against someone to put that person on trial. Your parents have probably been called to court before, as it's the duty of every American citizen to participate in this process. If a grand jury decides there *is* enough evidence, it will issue an indictment (a formal document charging someone of a crime), and a trial (the examination of evidence before a judge) may be held.

Right Against Double Jeopardy

This means that you can't be tried for the same crime more than once.

I plead the Fifth!

Right to Protect Oneself Against Self-Incrimination (Plead the Fifth)

When someone "pleads the Fifth" in court, that person is refusing to testify against him- or herself during a trial. *Testify* means to give evidence by speaking in court, so by testifying against yourself, you're basically acting as your own witness (someone who saw some or all of the crime). Why wouldn't people want to be their own witness in court? Well, sometimes people plead the Fifth because they're afraid something they say could potentially be used as evidence against them. This doesn't necessarily mean that the person is guilty and is trying to hide it (though sometimes, that's exactly what it means!). It could just mean they're afraid whatever they say will be misunderstood or misinterpreted. Other times people may plead the Fifth because they can't remember what happened, so they literally have nothing to say. Lawyers often tell clients to plead the Fifth because they don't want to risk their clients saying the wrong thing by accident, thus making themselves look guilty!

How Does This Affect Me?

If you're ever arrested and brought in for questioning, it is your right to plead the Fifth. Whatever you say to the officers can be used against you in court, so it's best not to say anything until a lawyer is present. You don't want to say anything wrong by accident or be baited into saying something that makes you sound guilty. After you speak to a lawyer, he or she will suggest how to proceed.

Right of Due Process

After people are arrested for a crime, they have the right to due process—a.k.a., a fair trial that follows certain rules.

Right to Eminent Domain

This means the government can't take your private property without paying you for it. This is also called the "takings clause."

Miranda Warning

The Miranda warning has to do with the Fifth and Sixth Amendments, but it's never mentioned by name in the Bill of Rights. It's named after the important Supreme Court case *Miranda v. Arizona* in 1966, in which the Court decided that officers must tell people their rights before taking them into police custody and questioning them. Those rights are:

★ **The right to remain silent (a.k.a., the right to plead the Fifth!)**

★ **The right to have an attorney (a lawyer, or someone who can defend them in court) present before and during the police questioning**

★ **The right, if they don't have enough money to pay an attorney, to have one appointed to them for free**

If the officer doesn't inform suspects of these rights before questioning them, anything the suspects say—even if it shows that they're guilty of a crime!—cannot be used against them in court.

THE SIXTH AMENDMENT

In all criminal prosecutions, the accused shall enjoy the right to a speedy and public trial, by an impartial jury of the State and district wherein the crime shall have been committed, which district shall have been previously ascertained by law, and to be informed of the nature and cause of the accusation; to be confronted with the witnesses against him; to have compulsory process for obtaining witnesses in his favor, and to have the Assistance of Counsel for his defence.

The Sixth Amendment protects the rights of people who have been accused of a crime and need a criminal trial.

The Framers wanted to make sure that people who were on trial did not receive unfair treatment or unfair imprisonment. Hence, they wrote the Sixth Amendment, which applies to criminal cases but not to civil ones. (Civil cases are disputes between organizations or regular private citizens like you and your friends, and they tend to involve someone suing someone else for money, or "damages.")

The idea here is that just because someone could be a criminal, doesn't mean that person should be treated as less than human. Without this amendment, you wouldn't have many rights at all if you needed to go to court.

The rights that are given under this amendment are *the rights to a speedy trial, a public trial, impartial jury, notice of accusation, confrontation, assistance of counsel, and self-representation.*

Did You Know?

The *defendant* is the suspect accused of a crime in a criminal trial. The defendant usually has an attorney for defense in court. The defendant's attorney gathers evidence to show the defendant is not guilty of a crime (this sometimes involves hiring a private investigator). This evidence could be witnesses or physical evidence (such as fingerprints, paint, or fibers). The defense also uses the police report to find holes or violations—such as unreasonable searches—in the case against the defendant. Finding small details like this could totally change the outcome of a trial. For instance, if the defendant's lawyer discovers that the prosecution obtained evidence in an unlawful way, then that evidence can't be used in court.

The *prosecution* is the attorney who is speaking on behalf of the government, defending the laws that the government created and bringing lawbreakers to justice! The prosecutor uses evidence from police and other experts to help support the case.

Right to a Speedy Trial

The Bill of Rights doesn't say exactly what *speedy* means, but this part of the Sixth Amendment stops the government from holding a suspect against his or her will while delaying a trial on purpose. In some states, defendants have a right to a trial in a certain number of days. Attorneys may suggest clients give up (or waive) this right, however, so that they have enough time to gather evidence to defend their clients.

Know Your Rights ★ 70

Right to a Public Trial

A public trial means the media—and regular everyday people like you—can be there to watch or record it. This right is necessary because it keeps the government from having secret, or potentially unfair or illegal, trials. Secret trials were actually common in Great Britain during the time that the Framers drafted the Bill of Rights, and they wanted to make sure it didn't become a thing here at home!

Right to an Impartial Jury

We know from the previous section that the job of a grand jury is to determine if a trial is even necessary. Once it's been decided that a trial *will*, in fact, take place—the role of a regular impartial jury (six to twelve members) is to listen to the evidence presented and to decide afterward if the defendant is guilty of the alleged crime or not. The word *impartial* here just means that the jury members are not biased—they don't already have opinions about the case or about general issues related to the case. When people are accused of a serious crime with a potential sentence lasting longer than six months, an impartial jury gives them a fair chance to present their side of the story. In criminal cases, the decision (guilty or not guilty) must be unanimous, meaning that everyone in the jury must agree. Otherwise, the trial must take place again with a different jury, made up of different people.

Think About It

Did you know that sometimes trials have to get moved to different towns in order to find impartial juries? Why do you think this might happen?

Right to Notice of Accusation

When people are arrested, they have the right to learn about the charges against them. Without this right, the government could lock people up for a long time without even bothering to tell them why!

Right to Confrontation

During a trial, the suspect has the right to confront—or question—witnesses who say they saw the crime. (In reality, it's usually the suspect's attorney who is doing the asking on the suspect's behalf.) Without this right, witnesses could say anything they wanted without anyone examining the statements to make sure they were true.

This right also relates to the use of physical evidence, like a letter or a photo, in a trial. The prosecution must allow the jury to see each piece of evidence, and the suspect's attorney is allowed to ask questions about it.

Right to Assistance of Counsel

The right to assistance of counsel means that all people accused of crimes can have an attorney to help them prove their case. If someone doesn't have enough money to pay an attorney, the government will give them a special kind of free attorney known as a public defender.

Right to Self Representation

People accused of crimes also have the right to not use an attorney at all—but if they choose this option, they must represent themselves in court instead. This can be a risky move, as you'd imagine. Most people who didn't go to law school don't have the skills, knowledge, and experience that attorneys do!

THE SEVENTH AMENDMENT

In Suits at common law, where the value in controversy shall exceed twenty dollars, the right of trial by jury shall be preserved, and no fact tried by a jury, shall be otherwise re-examined in any Court of the United States, than according to the rules of the common law.

The Seventh Amendment applies to federal civil cases instead of criminal ones. Remember, a civil case is a *noncriminal lawsuit* (for example, breaking a contract, getting a divorce, etc.). The Seventh Amendment guarantees that people involved in a civil case have a right to trial by jury instead of a trial with only a judge.

What Might a Civil Trial Look Like?

★ **Sally's car gets rear-ended by another driver as she's on her way to work. She decides to sue the person who hit her for money to pay for the damage to her beloved Audi®.**

★ Paperhead Fancy Paper Incorporated gets angry when Middlemucker Paper R Us starts using a new logo that looks suspiciously too much like Paperhead's logo. Paperhead decides to sue.

★ John Bee, a fourteen-year-old student, sues his school of violating his rights when the school suspends him for wearing a T-shirt speaking out against a local politician.

Civil cases go to trial in court, just like criminal ones. The party who files the case is called a plaintiff, and the one who the plaintiff is accusing of wrongdoing is the respondent (or defendant). Once there's a final judgment in favor of one of the parties, the case can't be tried again. (Remember how double jeopardy works?!)

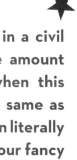

Did You Know?

The Seventh Amendment says that parties in a civil trial have a right to a jury—as long as the amount being sued for is more than $20. Back when this amount was decided on, $20 was worth the same as $400 is worth today. If this rule were still taken literally today, you could sue someone for breaking your fancy NERF™ gun! Today, though, federal courts won't even listen to a case when the amount in question is less than $75,000.

EIGHTH AMENDMENT

Excessive bail shall not be required, nor excessive fines imposed, nor cruel and unusual punishments inflicted.

The Eighth Amendment is a big one as far as the Bill of Rights goes. You've probably heard some of its wording before (*cruel and unusual punishment*) in the news, the movies, or even in debates at school.

This amendment limits what kinds of punishments the government can give to people accused or convicted of a crime. It pretty much states that *the punishment must fit the crime*. When the Framers wrote this, they wanted to protect people from being tortured, because some of the punishments that existed back in the day were pretty extreme (think whipping, branding, and ear cropping).

Excessive Bail

When people are accused of a serious crime, the judge may decide they need to stay in jail until they're proven innocent or found guilty. But sometimes the judge determines that they can get out before the trial if they—or their families—pay a certain amount of money (known as bail). If the person shows up for all necessary court appearances, the bail money will be returned. The amount of bail is based on how serious the crime is and how likely the person is to run away. In any case, not everyone has enough money to pay for bail. The Eighth Amendment says that the amount of bail can't be set so high that no person would reasonably be able to pay it. If a judge decides a person is very dangerous to a community, bail can be denied altogether so that the accused remains in jail until the trial.

Excessive Fines

Sometimes, when a person or organization is convicted of a crime—such as littering—they have to pay a fine to the government. The Eighth Amendment ensures that the fine can't be unreasonably high. (Imagine if you threw your empty can of soda on the ground and had to pay a fine of a million dollars for littering—that would be pretty unfair! Littering is not okay, but a fine of a million dollars is excessive.)

Cruel and Unusual Punishment

The *cruel and unusual punishment* part of the Eighth Amendment was there so that the government wouldn't commit acts of torture to punish people, like whipping them or tying them up in the town square.

But what else does *cruel and unusual punishment* include? Who decides? Often, the courts do.

The Eighth Amendment in Action: *Ingraham v. Wright*

In 1970, an eighth grader named James Ingraham was hit twenty times with a wooden paddle by his school principal. This was done as punishment when Ingraham didn't leave the stage of the school auditorium as soon as a teacher asked him to. Afterward, Ingraham and another student who had been punished in a similar way decided to sue the school because they felt their Eighth Amendment rights had been violated. But the Supreme Court decided that, because the Eighth Amendment was written to protect prisoners from torture rather than students from physical punishment, the paddling the students received did not violate the amendment (*Ingraham v. Wright*, 430 U.S. 651 [1977]).

The Death Penalty Debate

The death penalty (also known as capital punishment) is a huge part of the conversation surrounding the Eighth Amendment.

The death penalty is when the government orders someone to be killed as punishment for a very serious crime, usually murder. The Supreme Court has ruled that the death penalty is *not* considered cruel and unusual and is not a violation of the Eighth Amendment. Right now, thirty-two states allow it, and some people believe it is ethical for the government to punish certain crimes with this eye-for-an-eye method. But many people in the United States think that the death penalty is inhumane and are fighting for it to be abolished.

THE NINTH AMENDMENT

The enumeration in the Constitution, of certain rights, shall not be construed to deny or disparage others retained by the people.

The Ninth Amendment basically says that just because a certain right isn't listed in the Bill of Rights, that doesn't mean it doesn't exist or that it can't exist. (Did your mind just flip-flop trying to figure out what that means? It's confusing!)

Think about it like this: the Constitution is just one document—granted it's one *long* document but still only one. One document can't possibly cover all the needs of all the people—partly because those needs will inevitably change as time goes on and people change. The wording of this particular amendment is tricky, but the amendment itself is important. It means that just because a right isn't mentioned in the Constitution doesn't mean that Americans don't have that right. James Madison intended this amendment to be vague because he wanted to leave room for future generations to interpret the Constitution themselves. Think about all the court cases we've read about so far in which certain rights weren't mentioned in the Constitution and so people had to turn to the courts to figure them out. This amendment gives Americans the room to figure out those gray areas in which simply turning to the Constitution doesn't give cut-and-dried answers.

Here's a quick explanation on some of the terms used in the Ninth Amendment:

Your Handy-Dandy Ninth Amendment Vocab List

> *enumeration in the Constitution, of certain rights*
> **Enumeration means "an organized list." So here, the Ninth Amendment is referencing the full list of rights included in the Constitution.**

> *shall not be construed*
> **Construed means "how something is interpreted." So *shall not be construed* means "should not be understood as" or "should not be seen as."**

deny or disparage others retained by the people
Deny or disparage here means "to take away or minimize the importance of."

The Ninth Amendment in Action:
Griswold v. Connecticut

In the landmark 1965 Supreme Court case *Griswold v. Connecticut*, the Court ruled that there is an *implied* (not written out in words, but hinted at) right to privacy in the Constitution. At that time, birth control (devices or medications that people can use to help plan when or if they'll have a baby) was illegal in Connecticut. When

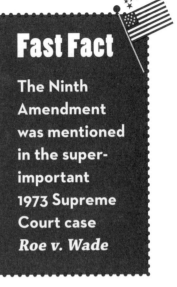

Fast Fact

The Ninth Amendment was mentioned in the super-important 1973 Supreme Court case *Roe v. Wade*

Estelle Griswold, a worker at the women's health clinic Planned Parenthood, was arrested for talking to clients about their family planning choices, she claimed that the state laws were violating people's rights to privacy within their marriages and their homes. The Court agreed, and birth control then became legal for married couples in Connecticut. Just because the right to privacy isn't specifically addressed in the Constitution doesn't mean that the government can withhold that right from people (*Griswold v. Connecticut*, 381 U.S. 479 [1965]).

Think About It

What are some of your favorite "other rights" that aren't mentioned in the Constitution but that every American citizen (including you!) has? (Perhaps you might want the right to binge-watch Netflix® for six hours at a time or the right to occasionally eat breakfast for dinner?)

THE TENTH AMENDMENT

The powers not delegated to the United States by the Constitution, nor prohibited by it to the States, are reserved to the States respectively, or to the people.

Because the Framers wanted to make sure the national government couldn't totally overpower the individual authority of the states, they drafted the Tenth Amendment. It may sound pretty similar to the Ninth Amendment, and it is, in a way. But the Tenth Amendment explains more clearly how powers are divided up between the states and the federal government.

"The powers delegated by the proposed Constitution to the federal government are few and defined. Those which are to remain in the State governments are numerous and indefinite."

—JAMES MADISON, ON THE TENTH AMENDMENT

As you know, the federal government is the *national* government. It's made up of Congress, the president, and the Supreme Court. The state governments are the individual governments of each and every state.

The federal government is the Big Kahuna when it comes to the powers it possesses under the Constitution, as well as the kinds of issues it deals with. It's concerned with large-scale issues of war and peace, trade and business, foreign policy, and more. In addition to the ones mentioned previously on page 26, some of the federal government's powers are to:

* ★ **coin money**

* ★ **regulate business between states**

* ★ **establish national banks**

* ★ **make treaties**

Individual state governments, on the other hand, are more concerned with the everyday lives of their local residents. There are so many people that live in the United States, the national government would have a really hard time taking care of everyone and addressing everyone's needs—not to mention just knowing what those needs even are! That's why state governments are so crucial; they're able to address the specific needs of the people in each particular state by focusing on issues such as local business regulations, traffic rules, and marriage and divorce laws. Some of the powers reserved by the states are to:

* ★ **make traffic laws**

* ★ **control education**

* ★ **hold elections**

* ★ **control business inside the state**

★ organize local police and fire departments

★ issue licenses, like drivers' licenses

★ make marriage and divorce laws

The state governments and the national government share the power to:

★ collect taxes

★ set up courts

★ create roads

★ make laws

★ borrow money . . . and more!

Think About It

Did you notice that the Tenth Amendment ends with the words *the people*—two of the very same (and very important) words that start the Constitution? Do you think this was a conscious decision on the Framers' part? Why?

PART THREE

More Amendments

Amendments 11–27: A Cheat Sheet

In the last section we discussed the importance of the Bill of Rights. Believe it or not, there are seventeen amendments that come *after* the Bill of Rights, too.

The Eleventh through Twenty-seventh Amendments focus on a huge range of topics. These amendments cover everything from slavery to alcohol consumption to taxes to voting rights.

In this section, we'll look at some of the most important amendments that come *after* the Bill of Rights. (We don't have space to go over every single one, and you might get bored if we tried! We're only going to discuss the ones that are most relevant to people today.)

Fast Fact

There hasn't been a new Constitutional amendment added since 1992—but that doesn't mean there won't be! The Framers designed the Constitution to be able to change with the times.

85

First, here's a cheat sheet so you get the gist of the Eleventh through Twenty-seventh Amendments:

ELEVENTH AMENDMENT
Discusses lawsuits against individual states.

TWELFTH AMENDMENT
Explains how the president and vice president get elected.

THIRTEENTH AMENDMENT
Abolishes slavery.

FOURTEENTH AMENDMENT
Covers the scope of civil rights.

FIFTEENTH AMENDMENT
Gives black men, including former slaves, the right to vote.

SIXTEENTH AMENDMENT
Allows Congress to collect income taxes.

SEVENTEENTH AMENDMENT
Lets citizens, as opposed to state governments, elect their senators.

EIGHTEENTH AMENDMENT
Prohibits the manufacturing or sale of alcohol (this was known as Prohibition).

NINETEENTH AMENDMENT
Gives women the right to vote.

TWENTIETH AMENDMENT
Sets limits on the number of years that the president and members of Congress can serve.

TWENTY-FIRST
AMENDMENT
Repeals *the Eighteenth Amendment* and the prohibition of alcohol (yes—this can happen!).

TWENTY-SECOND
AMENDMENT
Says presidents can't serve for more than two terms (eight years).

TWENTY-THIRD
AMENDMENT
Gives people in Washington, D.C., the right to vote in presidential elections. (Did you know that the District of Columbia is not considered a state? D.C. does not have representation in the Senate, and its one member in the House has very limited powers.)

TWENTY-FOURTH
AMENDMENT
Makes it illegal to make someone pay a tax in order to vote.

TWENTY-FIFTH
AMENDMENT
Establishes rules about what happens when a president dies while in office or can no longer do his or her job.

TWENTY-SIXTH
AMENDMENT
Gives eighteen-year-olds the right to vote.

TWENTY-SEVENTH
AMENDMENT
Limits the ability of Congress to give itself a pay raise.

A Closer Look

Now that you have a basic understanding of each amendment in the Constitution, let's go over some of the most important amendments in greater detail. Of course, all the amendments serve a good purpose, but the ones examined in this chapter have made huge impact on the lives of everyday people. Our society would look very different today if these amendments had not passed.

THE THIRTEENTH AMENDMENT
Section 1.

> *Neither slavery nor involuntary servitude, except as a punishment for crime whereof the party shall have been duly convicted, shall exist within the United States, or any place subject to their jurisdiction.*

Section 2.

> *Congress shall have power to enforce this article by appropriate legislation.*

At the start of the Civil War (which began in 1861), nearly four million people of African descent were being forced to work as slaves in the United States.

Back then, America was divided up by states that allowed slavery (slave states) and ones that didn't (free states). Most of the slave states were in the South. Slaves often lived with masters who were cruel and violent.

In the 1857 Supreme Court case *Dred Scott v. Sanford*, the Supreme Court ruled that slaves, former slaves, and their children were not citizens. Since they were considered property, the Court said, they didn't have the right to sue in court. This is important because it meant that, based on skin color alone, an entire group of people was unable to legally protect themselves. The Court also ruled that, even if slaves ran away to a free state where slavery was illegal, they were still considered slaves and had to return to their owners, should they be caught (*Dred Scott v. Sanford*, 60 U.S. 393 [1857]).

President Abraham Lincoln tried to change this while the Civil War (the war between Northern states and Southern states) was going on. In 1863, he issued his *Emancipation Proclamation*, declaring that slaves must be freed in all states. Leading up to the Civil War, there had already been disagreements within the country about how much power belonged to individual states versus how much power belonged to the national government. States in the South thought that the national government had gained too much control, and slavery was one of their major concerns. People in Southern states felt that it was their right to own slaves, and that the national government shouldn't be able to change that. Not willing to forgo this "right," the South threatened to secede, or leave the country, and this is what started the Civil War. It's important to remember that Lincoln's Proclamation wasn't purely based on his wish to abolish (get rid of) slavery; it was also a military action. Lincoln wanted more men to help fight in the Civil War on the side of the North, and his strategy was that the freed slaves could become soldiers. In any case, the Proclamation didn't take effect right away, and many people were confused about the status of freed slaves even after the Civil War ended in 1865. The same year the war ended, the Thirteenth Amendment was added to the Constitution, abolishing slavery nationwide.

Think About It

Even today, people have disagreements over what the Civil War was about. Some think it was obviously about slavery; others believe it was about states' rights. What are your thoughts?

Did You Know?

Even though the original Constitution never mentions the word *slavery*, there's evidence that slavery was alive and well during the time that the Constitution was drafted. Article I, Section 2, Clause 3 states that the number of Congress members per state should be based "on the whole Number of free Persons" and "three fifths of all other Persons." Slaves were considered "other Persons," and were only considered three-fifths of a person under this Article. This Clause was nicknamed the Three-Fifths Compromise.

Also, according to what became known as the Fugitive Slave Clause, Article IV, Section 2, Clause 3 states that "No person held to Service or Labour in one State" would be freed by escaping to another state. This part of the Constitution is clearly referring to slaves.

Unfortunately, just because the Thirteenth Amendment outlawed slavery didn't mean that people stopped trying to exercise power over the black community. In 1865–1866, after the amendment passed, some Southern states launched a new set of laws known as the Black Codes.

Applied to anyone with more than one black great-grandparent, the Black Codes made it illegal for black people to do certain things that white people could do. It set up separate court systems for black people, in which the sentences handed down were far more severe than they were for whites (for example, whipping for minor offenses).

The Black Codes made it easier to throw black people in jail, which was basically like enslaving them all over again.

Section 2 of the Thirteenth Amendment specifically lets Congress pass laws against practices that violate the amendment. For instance, in the 1970s, the Supreme Court decided that racial discrimination (treating people differently based on their skin color or race) by private schools went against the Thirteenth Amendment, so the practice was outlawed. This case occurred after two black students filed a lawsuit after they weren't admitted into private school because of their race (*Runyan v. McCrary*, 427 U.S. 160 [1976]).

Did You Know?

Just because slavery is no longer legal in America doesn't mean it's over! As of 2013, nearly 30 million people were reported to be living as slaves around the world (including in the U.S.). Human trafficking—transporting people from one country to another to force them to work—is a huge problem that many people are trying to stop.

If this bothers you, get involved! Write a letter to your representative and ask him or her to help. There are also plenty of antislavery organizations you can help raise money for.

THE FOURTEENTH AMENDMENT

Section 1.

All persons born or naturalized in the United States, and subject to the jurisdiction thereof, are citizens of the United States and of the State wherein they reside. No State shall make or enforce any law which shall abridge the privileges or immunities of citizens of the United States; nor shall any State deprive any person of life, liberty, or property, without due process of law; nor deny to any person within its jurisdiction the equal protection of the laws.

Section 2.

Representatives shall be apportioned among the several States according to their respective numbers, counting the whole number of persons in each State, excluding Indians not taxed. But when the right to vote at any election for the choice of electors for President and Vice-President of the United States, Representatives in Congress, the Executive and Judicial officers of a State, or the members of the Legislature thereof, is denied to any of the male inhabitants of such State, being twenty-one years of age, and citizens of the United States, or in any way abridged, except for participation in rebellion, or other crime, the basis of representation therein shall be reduced in the proportion which the number of such male citizens shall bear to the whole number of male citizens twenty-one years of age in such State.

Section 3.

No person shall be a Senator or Representative in Congress, or elector of President and Vice-President, or hold any office, civil or military, under the United States, or under any State, who, having previously taken an oath, as a member of Congress, or as an officer of the United States, or as a member of any State legislature, or as an executive or judicial officer of any State, to support the Constitution of the United States, shall have engaged in insurrection or rebellion against the same, or given aid or comfort to the enemies thereof. But Congress may by a vote of two-thirds of each House, remove such disability.

Section 4.

The validity of the public debt of the United States, authorized by law, including debts incurred for payment of pensions and bounties for services in suppressing insurrection or rebellion, shall not be questioned. But neither the United States nor any State shall assume or pay any debt or obligation incurred in aid of insurrection or rebellion against the United States, or any claim for the loss or emancipation of any slave; but all such debts, obligations and claims shall be held illegal and void.

Section 5.

The Congress shall have the power to enforce, by appropriate legislation, the provisions of this article.

If your eyes started glazing over just the tiniest bit while reading that, we don't blame you—the Fourteenth Amendment is the longest of all the constitutional amendments! It was ratified in 1868 and was written to protect the rights of the former slaves who were freed after the Civil War. There are a bunch of other issues that this amendment addresses as well:

★ **It defines what an American citizen is and which "privileges and immunities" come with U.S. citizenship.**

★ **It sets up rules about how the Bill of Rights applies to the states. (Before the Fourteenth Amendment was passed, the Bill of Rights *only* applied to the federal government—not to individual state governments!)**

★ **It guarantees *due process of law* by the state governments—we'll explain this shortly!**

★ **It guarantees equal protection to all people under the law.**

★ **It ensures that people who rebel against the United States can't take government office.**

Let's look a little more closely at some of the highlights of this amendment.

What's a Citizen?

The first section of the Fourteenth Amendment breaks down citizenship. It determines that citizenship belongs to *anyone who was born in the United States.* This overruled the earlier decision of *Dred Scott v. Sanford* and meant that former slaves who were born in the United States were now officially American citizens.

Fast Fact

When the Fourteenth Amendment was first ratified, it said that Native Americans were *not* citizens, which is pretty shocking—they were the *first* Americans, after all! This changed later when the Indian Citizenship Act of 1924 guaranteed citizenship to all indigenous (or native) Americans.

The first section says that a person's citizenship can't be taken away unless the person lied to get it or voluntarily gave it up. Plus, it ensures that children born in the United States are considered citizens even if their parents are not.

Privileges and Immunities

This section stops states from discriminating against citizens of other states or taking away rights that are given to them by the Constitution. Imagine if you were discriminated against in Colorado because you came from Texas—that would be pretty uncool!

Due Process

The due process section of the Fourteenth Amendment is similar to the due process section in the Fifth Amendment. Remember how the Fifth Amendment prevented the government from interfering with a suspect's right to a fair trial? While due process in the Fifth Amendment relates to the actions of the federal government, in the Fourteenth Amendment, it's related to state governments. In other words, state governments are also not allowed to interfere with a suspect's right to a fair trial.

The Supreme Court has also held that the Fourteenth Amendment protects not only the right to a fair trial if a state government tries to interfere with a person's rights to life, liberty, and property, but it also protects people's fundamental rights against interference by state government at any time. Fundamental rights are the ones included in the Bill of Rights, plus ones the Supreme Court has recognized, including the rights to

★ **interstate travel (travel between states)**

★ **parent one's children**

★ **privacy**

★ **self-defense**

★ **marriage**

Recently, the Supreme Court ruled that marriage was a fundamental right, so states can no longer interfere with same-sex couples' right to marry (*Obergefell v. Hodges*, 576 U.S.__ [2015]).

Equal Protection

The Fourteenth Amendment also grants "equal protection of laws" to every single person in America. This means that all people—no matter their age, race, sex, gender, or religion—must be treated the same way under the law. (Seems like a no-brainer.)

Fourteenth Amendment in Action:
Brown v. Board of Education of Topeka

In this historic 1954 civil rights case, Oliver L. Brown challenged a Kansas school board's policy of forcing black students to attend separate schools from their white peers. Before *Brown v. Board of Education* was decided, schools were allowed to separate students on the basis of race, as long as they provided equal facilities for each group. In reality, things were not equal at all. White schools had way better resources (better school supplies, better classroom conditions) than the black schools had.

Oliver L. Brown thought it was wrong that his seven-year-old daughter, Linda, had to walk six blocks to catch a school bus, then ride a mile to her black school instead of simply attending the white school in her neighborhood. The Supreme Court ended up deciding that this violated the equal-protection clause of the Fourteenth Amendment. The Court determined that no state could continue to separate students based on race, because separate facilities were automatically not equal (*Brown v. Board of Education,* 347 U.S. 483 [1954]).

Whole-Person Representatation

In the original Constitution, slaves were considered only three-fifths of a person when it came to deciding how many representatives each state would get. This was really unfair, because while slaves were not considered citizens, their population was used to help certain states have more representatives. The Fourteenth Amendment changed that so all people in the United States were considered whole persons.

Fast Fact

Section 4 of the Fourteenth Amendment also says that the federal government would not pay slave owners back for "losing" their slaves. When slavery was abolished, slave owners were required to free their slaves. Remember the "takings clause" of the Fifth Amendment, in which the government must pay people when it takes their property? Section 4 of the Fourteenth Amendment says that state and federal governments would *not* pay people for financial losses resulting from the loss of slave labor. Why? Hmmm. . . . Maybe because people are not property!

Rebellion

Section 3 of the Fourteenth Amendment says that people who rebel against the government can't hold a government office. For example, this section of the amendment was used to prevent Victor L. Berger—a man who spoke against the government's participation in World War I—from taking his seat in the House of Representatives in 1919.

THE FIFTEENTH AMENDMENT

Section 1.

The right of citizens of the United States to vote shall not be denied or abridged by the United States or by any State on account of race, color, or previous condition of servitude.

Section 2.

The Congress shall have power to enforce this article by appropriate legislation.

The Fifteenth Amendment, ratified in 1870, was created to protect people's right to vote, regardless of the color of their skin. (This only applied to men, though! Women of any race did not have the right to vote until the Nineteenth Amendment was ratified in 1920.)

Did You Know?

When a group of people is kept from voting, it's called being "disenfranchised." (This word technically means being deprived of power or deprived of a certain right or privilege.)

The Fifteenth Amendment was the third of the "Reconstruction Amendments" (the Thirteenth, Fourteenth, and Fifteenth Amendments) created to grant equality for oppressed black Americans. Before this, every state controlled its own voting procedures and could make its own rules about who could and couldn't vote.

As important as the Fifteenth Amendment was in trying to level the playing field for Americans of all races, many states still found ways to stop African-Americans from voting. Some states instituted a poll tax, which meant that certain people had to *pay* to vote. The rule was that people who had a grandfather who had voted in a previous election didn't have to pay this tax, which pretty much meant that white people never had to pay the tax. Black people always had to pay (because how could they possibly have a grandfather who voted in the previous election if they themselves just got the right to vote?). This was a sneaky and cruel way to make it difficult for black people to vote so that their opinions would continue to go unheard.

Some states also prevented black people from voting by making them pass literacy (reading) tests first. Although some black people had learned to read, many had not because they were former slaves who didn't receive an education. Furthermore, the white people giving these tests would often decide to pass or fail people for random and sometimes ridiculous reasons. Some states even started enforcing a rule in which only white people could vote in primary elections (an earlier election that chooses the candidates who will run against each other in a future election). In some cases, some white people even banded together to try to scare black people away from voting at all! The Ku Klux Klan, for example, is one organized white supremacy group that did this, in addition to committing many other hate crimes against black people. This racist group acts on the belief that white Christian people are better than people of other races and religions. Unfortunately, they are still active today.

Many years after the Fifteenth Amendment was ratified, the Voting Rights Act of 1965—known as an act to enforce the Fifteenth Amendment—finally made these kinds of poll taxes and literacy tests illegal, and made the promises of the Fifteenth Amendment come true.

Fast Fact

Even though the Fifteenth Amendment was ratified and made into a law that governed all the states in the nation in 1870, Tennessee didn't go on record as ratifying it until 1997—127 years later!

THE EIGHTEENTH AMENDMENT
Section 1.

After one year from the ratification of this article the manufacture, sale, or transportation of intoxicating liquors within, the importation thereof into, or the exportation thereof from the United States and all the territory subject to the jurisdiction thereof for beverage purposes is hereby prohibited.

Section 2.

The Congress and the several States shall have concurrent power to enforce this article by appropriate legislation.

Section 3.

This article shall be inoperative unless it shall have been ratified as an amendment to the Constitution by the legislatures of the several States, as provided in the Constitution, within seven years from the date of the submission hereof to the States by the Congress.

The Eighteenth Amendment, ratified in 1919, made it illegal to sell, manufacture, or transport alcohol in the United States. You might think it would have been a crime, then, for Uncle Joe or Aunt Lynette to have a glass of wine with dinner, right? Nope—the amendment only banned the *making and sale* of alcohol, not the *consumption* of it. Of course, the point was still to ban Uncle Joe and Aunt Lynette from having that glass of wine at dinner, because abolishing the making or selling of alcohol made it a lot harder for people to drink it!

The Eighteenth Amendment was introduced and eventually passed because of pressure from the temperance movement (in this case, *temperance* means to refrain from drinking alcohol).

The temperance movement was launched after more and more people across the country succumbed to alcoholism, which led to a rise in violence at home, family neglect, and people losing their jobs.

Folks who supported the temperance movement were called reformers. Many reformers were women who believed alcohol was hurting their families. (Susan B. Anthony, one of the major figures involved in the women's suffrage movement for women's right to vote, was a huge supporter of the temperance movement.)

Fast Fact

The ratification of the Eighteenth Amendment ushered in the historical period known as Prohibition (as in the prohibition, or banning, of alcohol), which lasted for thirteen years.

In the early 1900s, the Anti-Saloon League (saloons were pretty much just bars where alcohol was served) protested with speeches, ads, and demonstrations against the sale of alcohol.

Fast Fact

One of the most well known reformers involved in the Anti-Saloon League, Carrie Amelia Nation, was so passionate about the cause that she was actually known for vandalizing saloons!

This amendment seemed like a good idea for a while—alcohol consumption dropped, and people were being arrested less often. But a public resistance to forced abstinence (abstaining from alcohol means not drinking it) was growing, and people began violently rebelling against the law. They wanted to have the freedom to drink, and soon, they'd have their wish.

Did You Know?

During Prohibition, Eighteenth Amendment supporters tried to rewrite the Bible with all the references to alcohol cut out!

THE TWENTY-FIRST AMENDMENT

Section 1.

The eighteenth article of amendment to the Constitution of the United States is hereby repealed.

Section 2.

The transportation or importation into any State, Territory, or possession of the United States for delivery or use therein of intoxicating liquors, in violation of the laws thereof, is hereby prohibited.

Section 3.

This article shall be inoperative unless it shall have been ratified as an amendment to the Constitution by conventions in the several States, as provided in the Constitution, within seven years from the date of the submission hereof to the States by the Congress.

In 1933, the Twenty-first Amendment was ratified—and lo and behold, alcohol was once again legal to sell and make! This amendment is unique because it's the only amendment that has ever been passed to *reverse an earlier amendment*.

Even though there had been lots of support for Prohibition during the temperance movement, the law grew unpopular over time. Crime rates and violence soared as gangsters sold alcohol illegally, and the ban on making and selling alcohol proved tough to enforce.

Fast Fact

The day the Twenty-first Amendment was ratified— December 5, 1933—is known as Repeal Day.

But just because making and selling alcohol was legal again didn't mean every state had to jump back in. In fact, the second section of the Twenty-first Amendment gives states the right to determine their own rules on alcohol within state lines. For example, towns can choose to remain "dry," or alcohol-free, and ban sales of alcoholic beverages. So even though the Twenty-first Amendment repealed (undid) the Eighteenth Amendment alcohol ban, it wasn't like the Twenty-first Amendment forced all states to start selling alcohol. Today, each state has unique laws regarding the sale of alcohol. In many states, liquor stores are closed on Sundays, but this isn't the case nationwide.

"What America needs now is a drink."
—PRESIDENT FRANKLIN D. ROOSEVELT, AFTER THE EIGHTEENTH AMENDMENT WAS REPEALED

THE NINETEENTH AMENDMENT

The right of citizens of the United States to vote shall not be denied or abridged by the United States or by any State on account of sex.

Congress shall have power to enforce this article by appropriate legislation.

Women and men deserve equal rights—right? You may think this is obvious, which is why it's pretty shocking to remember that most women in America actually couldn't vote in elections until 1920! (Before that, some states gave women the right to vote, but most didn't.)

Although women had been fighting for the right to vote since the mid-1800s, they weren't legally permitted to cast a ballot until after the Nineteenth Amendment was ratified in 1920. The movement of people organizing for women's right to vote was called *women's suffrage*, and the people involved in it were known as *suffragettes*. It was in 1848, at the Seneca Falls Convention—the first women's rights convention in the United States!—that activists first gathered to discuss the state of women's rights.

Did You Know?

At the Seneca Falls Convention, organizers Elizabeth Cady Stanton and Lucretia Mott revealed a document they'd drafted, called the Declaration of Sentiments. It was similar to the Declaration of Independence, but it specifically dealt with women's rights. It demanded women's right to vote, equal education, and more.

Elizabeth Cady Stanton, Lucy Stone, and Susan B. Anthony were some of the most well-known suffragettes, but tons of other women played a huge part, too, including African-American activists such as Sojourner Truth, Ida B. Wells, and Anna Julia Cooper. (There were also a few men, such as famous abolitionist and writer Frederick Douglass, who were important to the cause.)

Now, in view of this entire disfranchisement of one-half the people of this country, their social and religious degradation . . . we insist that they have immediate admission to all the rights and privileges which belong to them as citizens of the United States.

—DECLARATION OF SENTIMENTS, SENECA FALLS CONVENTION, 1848

The fight for women's suffrage was long and hard. Many men really did not want to give women the right to vote. Senator Aaron Sargent first introduced the Nineteenth Amendment way back in 1878, but Congress struck it down. Congress considered it again in 1914, and it passed in the House of Representatives, but failed in the Senate!

President Woodrow Wilson, who was originally against women's suffrage but later changed his mind, called Congress to vote on it again in 1918, and it finally passed. Women were allowed to vote nationwide at last. *Whew.* Took the government long enough!

The amendment was formally adopted on August 18, 1920, and later that year, women in many states voted for the very first time.

> **"In this denial of the right to participate in government, not merely the degradation of woman and the perpetuation of a great injustice happens, but the maiming and repudiation of one-half of the moral and intellectual power of the government of the world."**
>
> **—FREDERICK DOUGLASS, AUTHOR, ABOLITIONIST, AND ONE OF THE FEW MEN PRESENT AT THE SENECA FALLS CONVENTION**

It's important to note, though, that many black women were still disenfranchised even after they got the legal right to vote in 1920. State laws and rampant racism (unfairness or hatred toward someone based on race)—especially in the South—prevented many women of color from being able to wield their power at the ballot box. This changed when the Voting Rights Act of 1965 passed.

THE TWENTY-SIXTH AMENDMENT
Section 1.

The right of citizens of the United States, who are eighteen years of age or older, to vote shall not be denied or abridged by the United States or by any State on account of age.

Section 2.

The Congress shall have the power to enforce this article by appropriate legislation.

The Twenty-sixth Amendment lowered the voting age to eighteen. It had been twenty-one in most states before that.

During World War II, President Franklin D. Roosevelt lowered the draft age to eighteen, meaning that men eighteen years old could be drafted to serve in the war. (Being drafted means being forced to fight in a war, even if you don't want to.) Many people—especially young people—thought that it wasn't fair for the government to force people to fight in a war and die for their country while not even giving them the right to vote. They believed the voting age should be lowered to eighteen, to match the draft age.

Did You Know?

"Old enough to fight, old enough to vote" was a common slogan among youth activists fighting to lower the voting age in the 1940s.

President Dwight Eisenhower agreed. He was the first president to support lowering the voting age, and he spoke about it in a speech he gave in 1954. Despite this, the voting age remained stuck at twenty-one, and eighteen-year-olds

Fast Fact

The Twenty-sixth Amendment passed faster than any other amendment in U.S. history!

continued to be drafted in wars, including the Vietnam War (which lasted a whopping twenty years from 1955 to 1975). Finally, in 1971, Congress passed the Twenty-sixth Amendment, forcing *all states* to allow people as young as eighteen to cast their ballot in every election!

Think About It

If it were up to you, what would the voting age be? Do you think kids under age eighteen should be able to vote? Why or why not?

PART FOUR
What N★w?

Wrapping Up...

There wasn't enough space in this book to explore every amendment in the Constitution, but one of the cool things about the Constitution is that you can read it online anytime. And you can visit the National Archives, in Washington, D.C., where the original document is preserved. It's pretty amazing to see it up close!

If you're interested in American politics, there are many ways to get involved. Start a political science club at your school, or ask your journalism teacher if you can write a column about politics in the school paper. Take action to be an informed citizen by keeping up with the news and discussing current events with people who have views that differ from your own. You may not be old enough to vote, but you *can* call your senator or representative and speak with a staffer about changes you'd like to see in your state or community. You can also join or even organize a protest or march that gives voice to a cause that you believe in. Who knows? Maybe one day you'll run for office, and then you'll be the one helping to make our country a better place for everyone.

America certainly isn't perfect; our society still grapples with racism, sexism (unfairness or hatred toward someone based on gender), violence, and more. There's still a lot of work to do, but without the Constitution, we wouldn't have the rights, privileges, and freedoms we have today.

Learn More

Books to Read

Furi-Perry, Ursula. *Constitutional Law for Kids: Discovering the Rights and Privileges Granted by the U.S. Constitution.* Chicago, IL: American Bar Association, 2013.

JusticeLearning.org. *The United States Constitution: What It Says, What It Means.* Oxford, UK: Oxford University Press, 2005.

Sobel J.D., Syl. *How The U.S. Government Works.* Hauppauge, NY: Barron's Educational Series, 2012.

Sobel J.D., Syl. *The Bill of Rights: Protecting Our Freedom Then and Now.* Hauppage, NY: Barron's Educational Series, 2008.

Sobel J.D., Syl. *Presidential Elections and Other Cool Facts.* Hauppauge, NY: Barron's Education Series, 2016.

Websites to Visit

America's Founding Documents
Read transcripts of the Declaration of Independence, the Constitution, and the Bill of Rights, and also view images of the original paper documents.

https://www.archives.gov/founding-docs

Famous Speeches
Get your headphones ready! Listen to famous and important speeches given by American leaders such as Martin Luther King Jr., John F. Kennedy, and Barack Obama.

https://www.wyzant.com/resources/lessons/history/hpol/

News for Kids
Whether it's politics, sports, or science, use this site to stay in the know about current events.

http://htekidsnews.com/

Glossary

Abolish: to get rid of or make something illegal, such as slavery

Activist: a person who takes action to change things in the world that they believe are wrong or unfair

Alleged: a claim that someone has done something wrong or illegal

Amend: to change something that someone previously said or wrote

Amendment: a change in writing or in a statement

Article: a section of the Constitution

Bail: a temporary release from prison of someone awaiting trial, in exchange for payment of money that will be returned if the accused shows up for court appearances

Biased: unreasonably favoring certain ideas or people over other ones

Bill: a draft of a proposed law

Bill of Rights: the first ten amendments to the Constitution, involving people's individual rights

Bribery: offering money or a promise of some sort in order to get someone to do something

Cabinet: a group of high-ranking government officials who assist the president in doing things required by the executive branch of the government

Censor: to limit someone's speech, writing, performance, or art

Citizen: a legal resident of a particular country

Civil: relating to the needs and concerns of ordinary citizens

Civil trial: a trial in which one party (the plaintiff) argues that another (the defendant) has failed to carry out their end of a bargain, such as not paying for a service after it has been completed

Colony: a country or area under full or partial control of another country, usually one that is far away

Congress: the legislative branch of the government, made up of two groups: the House of Representatives and the Senate

Convicted: found guilty of a crime

Court: a space controlled by one or more judges, where trials and other legal matters take place

Crime: an illegal activity that can be prosecuted in court and punished under the law

Criminal trial: a trial in which the government, or, in rare cases, an individual (the prosecution), accuses another person (the defendant) of a crime

Delegate: an elected representative, usually one sent to a conference to represent the people in his or her area

Delinquency: relating to a minor (someone under the age of eighteen) who has broken the law

Democracy: a government, as we have in the United States, in which the people of the country have the power to make decisions, usually by voting in elections

Discrimination: different treatment—usually worse—toward another person or group of people, often due to their race, gender, sexual orientation, age, country of origin, or religion

Due process: a constitutional guarantee that laws be reasonable, that legal proceedings be fair, and that individuals have a right to be heard before the government can take away their life, freedom, or property

Elect: to choose someone for a position of power by voting for them

Election: an organized event in which people elect someone to a position of power by voting for them

Executive branch: the part of the government that enforces the laws put in place by the legislative branch and interpreted by the judicial branch

Evidence: facts, objects, and information used to prove whether a belief is true or false

Federal: relating to the government at the national level

Federalism: a mixed form of government, where power is shared between the national government and individual state governments

Founder: a person who helps create an organization or a government

Framer: a person who helped write the original draft of the United States Constitution

Government: a formal system intended to protect and regulate people in a community

Grand Jury: a group of people who examine accusations against a person who has been arrested for a crime, to determine whether there is enough evidence for the person to be charged and possibly sent to trial

House of Representatives: a group of elected officials who make up a portion of Congress, and who, along with the Senate, create laws

Idealistic: goals that strive toward perfection

Illegal: against the law

Impeachment: an accusation of wrongdoing against the president

Inhumane: cruel or extremely unfair

Jury: a group of people (usually twelve) chosen to weigh evidence in a trial and decide whether someone is innocent or guilty of a crime

Lawful: actions or activities done according to the law

Legal: relating to the law, or within what the law allows

Legislative branch: the lawmaking branch of the U. S. government, composed of two groups: the House of Representatives and the Senate

National: relating to the whole country

Obscenity: conduct that most people would find extremely offensive

Political: relating to the government or politics

Politics: relating to the government and its activities

President: the elected leader of the United States and head of the Executive branch of government

Probable cause: a logical belief, based on evidence, that a crime most likely has been, is being, or is about to be committed

Race: a group of people united by the same skin color and sometimes also by the same history, language, and culture

Racial discrimination: unjust treatment toward another person because of the person's skin color or race, also known as racism

Ratify: to sign or formally state that an agreement, such as a treaty, is official

Reasonable suspicion: a reasonable belief—more than a guess or a hunch, but less that probable cause— that a crime has been, is being, or will be committed

Repeal: to cancel a law

Senate: the group of appointed officials with more power than the House of Representatives who make up part of Congress and create laws

Sexism: discrimination or unfair treatment toward another gender based on the belief that one's own gender is superior

Social justice: sharing money, opportunities, and privileges in a fair way across society

Society: people who live in a particular country or area and share laws and similar customs

Suffrage: the right to vote in elections

Suffragette: a woman who protests for the right to vote

Tax: a charge that people must pay to support government activities and programs

Treason: the crime of betraying one's country, often by attempting to kill the leader or overthrow the government

Treaty: a formal agreement between two countries or governments

Trial: an examination of evidence before a judge, and usually a jury, to determine if someone is guilty of a criminal or civil offense

United States Supreme Court: the highest court in the United States, composed of eight associate justices and one chief justice

Unlawful: illegal

Veto: the president's constitutional power to stop or slow down the process of a bill becoming a law

Vice president: the head of the Senate and the person who takes over when the president is unable to fulfill his or her duties

Witness: a person who saw an event, such as a crime or injury, occur

Index

landmark ruling on, 32, 99

voting and. *See* Voting rights

Civil trials, about, 73–74

Civil War, slavery and, 90–91, 96

Clinton, Bill, 27

Confrontation, right to, 72

Congress, 23–27. *See also* Laws

    House of Representatives, 23–24, 25–26, 41

    how laws are created, 24–25

    impeachment power, 25–26, 27

    as legislative branch, 23–27

    other powers of, 26

    Senate, 23–24, 25, 26, 27, 32

Constitution

    American Revolution and, 14–15

    Articles and amendments explained, 20. *See also* Amendments; Articles (Constitution)

    changing nature of, 21

    Declaration of Independence and, 14, 20

    delegates, Framers and, 15, 16

    durability of, 21

    as highest law in the land, 20, 33

    as official, ratification of, 33

    origins of, reasons for, 13–15

    parts explained, 18–21

    powers not delegated to. *See* Tenth Amendment

    Preamble explaining purpose of, 18–19

    purpose/function of, 20

    reading and taking action, 115

    rights not mentioned in. *See* Ninth Amendment

    "We the People . . ." and, 18, 19, 82

    what to do from here, 115–116

    who created it, 15–17

    why it was created, 13–15

Constitutional Convention, 15–16, 90

Counsel, right to assistance of, 72–73

Court, rights related to. *See* Fifth Amendment; Sixth Amendment; Seventh Amendment

Criminal trials. *See* Fifth Amendment; Sixth Amendment

D

Davis v. United States, 60

Death penalty, 77

Declaration of Independence, 14, 20

Declaration of Sentiments, 109

Defendants, 70, 71

Departments, cabinet and, 28–29, 30

Division of power

    about: overview of, 23

    executive branch, 28–30. *See also* President

    federal vs. state power, 33

    judicial branch, 31–32

    legislative branch. *See* Congress

Double jeopardy, right against, 66

Douglass, Frederick, 109, 110

Dred Scott v. Sanford, 90, 96

Due process, right of, 68

E

Eighth Amendment, 75–77

Emancipation Proclamation, 90–91

Eminent domain, right to ("takings clause"), 68, 100

Enumeration in Constitution, Ninth Amendment, 77–80

Equality, Declaration of Independence on, 20

Equal protection, 94, 98–99

Executive branch, 28–30. *See also* President

Executive Office of the President (EOP), 28

F

Federal, defined, 12

Federalism, 33

Fifth Amendment, 64–68

    Miranda warning and, 68

    right against double jeopardy, 66

    right of due process, 68

    right of self-incrimination protection, 66–67

    right to eminent domain ("takings clause), 68, 100

    right to grand jury, 64, 65

    wording of, 64–65

Soldiers, quartering of, 58–59
Speech, freedom of, 49–52
Stanton, Elizabeth Cady, 109
States, due process of law by, 96, 97–98
States, powers/rights of, 33, 80–82
Supreme Court
    cases heard by, 31, 32
    constitutionality of laws and, 31
    judicial branch and, 31–32
    justices on, 32
    roles of, 31
Supreme Court cases. *See also specific cases*
    Black Codes case, 92–93
    cruel and unusual punishment case, 76–77
    freedom of religion cases, 46–47
    freedom of speech cases, 50–51
    freedom of the press cases, 52–53
    landmark ruling on civil rights, 32, 99
    Ninth Amendment case, 79
    search and seizure cases, 58–63
    slaves' rights case, 90

T

Takings clause (eminent domain), 68, 100
Temperance movement. *See* Alcohol, outlawing and legalization of
Tenth Amendment, 80–82
Third Amendment, 58–59

Thirteenth Amendment, 89–93. *See also* Slavery
Three-Fifths Compromise, 92. *See also* Whole-person representation
Tinker v. Des Moines, 50–51
Trial-related rights, civil cases, 73–74
Trial-related rights, criminal cases. *See* Fifth Amendment; Sixth Amendment

U

United States v. Robinson, 60

V

Vernonia School District v. Acton, 62–63
Veto power, 25, 29
Vice president, 24, 28, 29
Voting rights
    for citizens eighteen or older, 110–112
    regardless of race, color, previous condition of servitude, 101–103
    regardless of sex, 108–110
    for women of color, 110

W

Washington, George, 14, 30
Whole-person representation, 100
Wisconsin v. Yoder, 46–47
Witnesses, right to confront, 72
Women's suffrage, Nineteenth Amendment and, 108–110